UNLOCKING HAPPINESS

A 28-Day Journey to Defeat Depression, Freakout, Anxiety and Triggers

Emily Williams, PH.D.

Copyright 2023 © Emily Williams

This book is a work of non-fiction. The opinions expressed in this book are those of the author alone and do not necessarily reflect those of the publisher, which disclaims any responsibility for them.

INTRODUCTION

Sarah had reached her breaking point. Her life had been taken over by depression and anxiety, making each day a fight to survive. She felt as though she were drowning in a sea of hopelessness.

Sarah came across a post from a friend while lazily perusing social media one dismal afternoon. It was a touching testimonial about how "Unlocking Happiness" had changed their lives in just 28 days. Intrigue and yearning for a change, Sarah ordered the book immediately.

She sensed a gleam of optimism as she read through its pages. The 28-day journey appeared to be her lifeline. She did the workouts religiously every day. She began practicing mindfulness, cultivating self-compassion, and establishing a support network.

Sarah could sense a shift within herself week after week. The darkness faded as she learned to challenge her negative ideas and cope with her triggers. She embraced appreciation and rediscovered a feeling of purpose she'd long lacked.

Sarah was a different person by the end of the 28 days. The book provided her with the tools to overcome depression and anxiety and unlocked the happiness she had thought she would never experience again. She stepped into a brighter, more hopeful future with increased strength.

You, like Sarah, might feel better after the process. All you have to do is follow the guidelines in this book, and your path to healing will begin.

It won't always be easy, but Sarah's experience demonstrates the strength of resilience and the effectiveness of the 28-day journey. You, too, may find the strength to face each day with renewed optimism.

As you read the chapters, you'll uncover insights and techniques that worked for Sarah and many others. You'll learn to detect and control the tendencies contributing to your depression and anxiety. This book would teach you mindfulness which allows you to discover serenity in the present moment, breaking free from the bonds of stress and regret.

Self-compassion will become second nature, and you'll see the transformational power of a robust support network. You'll learn how to tackle your triggers and battle negative beliefs.

The shadows of depression and anxiety will gradually fade each week like clouds parting after a storm. You'll notice a significant transformation in your well-being as you embrace appreciation and rediscover your purpose.

By the end of the 28 days, you'll be standing on the verge of a brighter future, just like Sarah, confident in your abilities and resilience to sustain your newfound happiness. Remember, your healing journey begins when you take the first step and commit to the process indicated on these pages.

CHAPTER ONE

Understanding Depression and Anxiety

On the first day of your path to unlocking happiness and fighting depression and anxiety, it is vital you take this important step of learning about the two terrible opponents you are against. This fundamental information would serve as your compass, guiding you through the treacherous terrain ahead.

Although depression and anxiety are sometimes used interchangeably, they are distinct mental health illnesses with distinct characteristics. Understanding these disparities is critical for designing a personalized healing strategy.

Depression is characterized by a loss of interest in previously pleasurable things to the depressed person, as well as persistent sadness and hopelessness. It's like a huge fog hanging over one's life, making even the simplest activities appear impossible. Sarah, for instance, noticed she could not eat and sleep and was usually exhausted.

Conversely, anxiety is a persistent feeling of concern, fear, and dread about the future. It can range from minor anxiety to terrifying panic episodes. It frequently causes a condition of hyperarousal, with symptoms such as racing thoughts, restlessness, and even bodily signs such as sweating and palpitations.

Understanding these concepts would enable you to differentiate between depression and anxiety. Chronic unhappiness and lack of motivation were symptoms of depression, while racing thoughts and continual worries were symptoms of anxiety.

Common Symptoms

With a clearer understanding of the two conditions, you can delve deeper into their common symptoms. Knowledge is power, and in this case, knowing what to look out for is the first step in your battle against depression and anxiety.

Persistent Sadness: Depression is characterized by an unwavering sense of sadness, hopelessness, and emptiness. It frequently lasts weeks or months, interfering with daily living.

Loss of Interest: One of the defining signs of depression is loss of interest or pleasure in formerly enjoyable activities. You may realize that your hobbies had lost their appeal long ago

Fatigue: Even after a full night's sleep, depression can leave people physically and psychologically exhausted. This weariness can make everyday chores seem impossible.

Appetite Changes: Recognized that depression could impact appetite, resulting in dramatic weight changes. When depressed, some people eat more, while others lose their appetite.

Sleep Disturbance: Insomnia or excessive sleepiness throughout the day might be associated with depression. You must identify inconsistent sleep patterns which could be a contributing factor to your weariness.

Irritability: Irritability and restlessness can accompany depression, negatively impacting personal relationships. You must realize that short temper can strain your relationships.

Anxiety brought symptoms, including excessive worrying, restlessness, and a constant sense of being on edge.

Physical Symptoms: Both depression and anxiety can have physical manifestations. When anxious, you might notice your heart would speed up and have muscle tension.

You must realize these are not isolated episodes but part of a bigger framework. You are not alone in this fight; millions of individuals throughout the world experienced similar issues daily.

With this information, I believe you are better prepared to face the journey ahead. You now have a better understanding of your opponents, depression, and anxiety and now ready to embark on your 28-day quest to unlock happiness and recover your life.

CHAPTER TWO

Exploring Happiness from a Scientific Perspective

The pursuit of happiness, a state of being that is both elusive and highly sought after, has long fascinated philosophers, intellectuals, and scientists.

Happiness is generally defined scientifically as a subjective, positive emotional state marked by emotions of joy, contentment, and satisfaction with one's life. It is a state that goes beyond momentary pleasures to a deeper sense of well-being and fulfillment.

The Role of Brain Chemistry in Happiness

The brain's basis of happiness is one of the most fascinating parts of it. Neuroscientists have made ground-breaking discoveries about the brain's role in happiness generation. Neurotransmitters like serotonin, dopamine, and endorphins play pivotal roles in maintaining mental and emotional health.

Serotonin, sometimes known as the "feel-good" neurotransmitter, helps to stabilize mood and adds to general happiness. Dopamine, on the other hand, is linked to pleasure and reward. When we have a joyful experience, our brain releases dopamine, reinforcing our desire to repeat those behaviors.

Endorphins, another neurotransmitter, are natural pain relievers and mood boosters. They are released during physical exertion, laughter, and even specific foods, resulting in pleasure and a sensation of well-being.

Understanding the role of these neurotransmitters can help us understand why certain activities and experiences can boost our mood and lead to happiness. It also emphasizes balancing these substances through lifestyle choices and self-care activities.

The Relationship Between Happiness and Mental Health

Happiness and mental health have a strong and reciprocal relationship. Depression and anxiety are two prevailing mental health problems that can drastically reduce one's ability for happiness.

A continuous sense of enjoyment, on the other hand, can boost mental resilience and act as a preventive factor against the development of these illnesses.

Low serotonin levels, for example, are common in depression and can lead to chronic emotions of sadness and hopelessness.

Understanding the neurochemical foundation of depression allows us to comprehend the necessity of therapies such as medication and psychotherapy that aim to restore serotonin equilibrium.

Happiness, on the other hand, can be a great barrier against stress and misfortune. Positive emotions and a general sense of well-being help us deal with life's problems. As we will see in this book, cultivating happiness through diverse activities can be a preventative step against the onset of mental health difficulties and contribute to general emotional resilience.

Happiness Can Be Cultivated

The idea that happiness can be grown and nurtured is one of the most empowering insights in the science of positive psychology. While genetic predisposition and life circumstances surely play a role in establishing our baseline happiness, we have control over a large chunk of it.

This concept questions the widely held belief that happiness is a destination to be attained, a fixed state of being that some are privileged to have while others are not.

Rather, it implies that pleasure is a skill that can be cultivated and grown by deliberate practices and mindset modifications.

This book will look at several evidence-based approaches and exercises for cultivating happiness. Positive psychology, mindfulness, and cognitive-behavioral therapy are all used in these activities. You can gradually adjust your baseline of happiness and experience a more lasting sense of well-being by adopting them into your daily life.

Finally for this chapter, happiness science indicates that this complex feeling is firmly rooted in our brain chemistry and is intricately linked to our mental health. Understanding the neurological foundation of happiness enables us to recognize the importance of interventions that target these pathways.

Furthermore, the notion that happiness can be developed gives people optimism and empowerment to improve their well-being. The next chapters will examine practical techniques for realizing this potential and embarking on a transformative path to happiness.

CHAPTER THREE

Overview of the 28-Day Journey

Understanding the structure of the journey, daily tasks, and goals is critical in this transformative journey to combat sadness and anxiety while unleashing happiness. This chapter establishes the reader's commitment and involvement in the next weeks.

The 28-day journey is a well-planed roadmap divided into four distinct weeks, each with its purpose. Each week builds on the one before it, taking you on a journey of self-discovery and personal improvement.

Week-1 Self-awareness

In the first week of our 28-day journey towards defeating depression and anxiety while unlocking happiness, we lay the essential groundwork for your transformation. This week is dedicated to building a solid foundation that will support your progress throughout the journey.

We'll detail the activities and practices for Week 1, emphasize the significance of self-awareness, provide tips on setting achievable goals, and share personal stories and illustrate the power of this foundational work.

The following are the important activities and practices to look forward to during this foundational week:

Daily Journaling: Begin each day by writing down your thoughts and feelings. Consider your current mental state, feelings, and any trends you've seen or experience. Journaling is an effective practice for increasing self-awareness.

Mindfulness Meditation: Incorporate short periods of mindfulness meditation into your everyday practice. These quiet moments will help you become more aware of your thoughts and feelings.

Goal-setting: Establish attainable goals for this week. These objectives should be explicit, measurable, and achievable. They can be about self-care, personal growth, or any other aspect of your life you want to improve.

Gratitude Practice: At the end of each day, write down three things you're grateful for. This exercise promotes happiness and directs your attention to the positive aspects of life.

Self-Reflection: Set aside time for self-reflection, asking yourself questions such as, "What brings me joy?" "What are my strengths?" and "What areas of my life need improvement?"

Positive Affirmations on an Everyday Basis: Incorporate positive affirmations into your everyday routine. These statements can be used to counteract negative self-talk and increase self-esteem.

The Value of Self-Awareness

Self-awareness is the foundation of personal development and emotional well-being. It necessitates a thorough grasp of your thoughts, feelings, behaviors, and motives. We emphasize self-awareness in Week 1 since it is the foundation upon which you will build enduring happiness.

You can use self-awareness to:

1. Recognize negative thinking or self-sabotage patterns.
2. Recognize sadness and anxiety triggers.
3. Recognize your talents and weaknesses.
4. Make well-informed judgments that are consistent with your values and aspirations.

By growing self-awareness, you can respond to life's obstacles more consciously and constructively. It allows you to break free from automatic, habitual responses and regain control of your emotional well-being.

How to Set Achievable Goals

Setting objectives is an essential part of human development and advancement. However, creating reasonable and achievable goals is critical, especially in the early stages of your journey. Here are some suggestions for setting goals in Week 1:

Start small: Begin with small, reasonable goals that you can complete within a week. As your confidence grows, you can set more aggressive goals in the coming weeks.

Be Specific: Clearly define your objectives. Instead of a broad objective like "be happier," be specific, such as "practice gratitude daily" or "engage in a 10-minute mindfulness meditation each morning."

Measure Progress: Determine how you will track your progress. This could be keeping a notebook, utilizing a monitoring tool, or simply reflecting on your daily activities.

Maintain your flexibility: Life is unpredictable, and unexpected obstacles can come. Be willing to change your goals, if necessary, without becoming disheartened.

Acknowledge and praise even the smallest accomplishments. This inspiring encouragement will motivate you to continue.

Examples of SMART goals which you Could Set

It is important you set SMART (Specific, Measurable, Achievable, Realistic, and Time-bound). Note that these examples are proven life experience that have benefited previous readers.

Some examples of SMART goals consist of the following:

Goal 1: Morning Routine

Specific: Wake up at 7 AM every day.

Measurable: You can track the time you wake up each morning.

Achievable: Adjust your bedtime to ensure you get enough sleep.

Realistic: Setting a consistent wake-up time is manageable.

Time-bound: Implement this within a week.

Goal 2: Daily Exercise

Specific: Walk briskly for 20 minutes every day.

Measurable: Track your daily walk duration.

Achievable: Start with a short walk and gradually increase it.

Realistic: A 20-minute walk is manageable for most people.

Time-bound: Start today and continue for a month.

Goal 3: Mindfulness Practice

Specific: Meditate for 5 minutes each morning.

Measurable: Use a timer to track your meditation time.

Achievable: Start with a short duration and increase it over time.

Realistic: 5 minutes is a realistic starting point.

Time-bound: Begin this practice tomorrow.

Goal 4: Gratitude Journal

Specific: Write down three things you're grateful for every night.

Measurable: Track the number of entries in your journal.

Achievable: It's a simple practice that can be done daily.

Realistic: Listing three things is manageable.

Time-bound: Start tonight and continue for at least three weeks.

Goal 5: Connect with Others

Specific: Reach out to a friend or family member every day.

Measurable: Keep a record of your daily connections.

Achievable: Sending a text or making a quick call is feasible.

Realistic: Daily communication is manageable.

Time-bound: Start immediately and continue indefinitely.

Goal 6: Limit Screen Time

Specific: Limit daily screen time to 2 hours.

Measurable: Track your daily screen usage.

Achievable: Gradually reduce screen time to this limit.

Realistic: 2 hours is a reasonable target.

Time-bound: Implement this within a week.

Goal 7: Healthy Eating

Specific: Include a serving of vegetables in one meal per day.

Measurable: Keep track of meals with vegetables.

Achievable: Incorporating veggies into a meal is achievable.

Realistic: A single serving is manageable.

Time-bound: Start with your next meal.

Goal 8: Hydration

Specific: Drink 8 glasses of water daily.

Measurable: Keep a tally of glasses consumed.

Achievable: Spread water intake throughout the day.

Realistic: 8 glasses are a healthy target.

Time-bound: Begin immediately and maintain daily.

Goal 9: Bedtime Routine

Specific: Establish a bedtime routine with calming activities.

Measurable: Track adherence to your routine.

Achievable: Choose relaxing activities before sleep.

Realistic: A calming bedtime routine is feasible.

Time-bound: Start tonight and continue indefinitely.

Goal 10: Limit Caffeine and Alcohol

Specific: Reduce caffeine intake to one cup per day.

Measurable: Keep track of daily caffeine consumption.

Achievable: Gradually decrease your caffeine intake.

Realistic: One cup of caffeine is manageable.

Time-bound: Start tomorrow and maintain for a month

Personal Stories of Previous Readers

To demonstrate the importance of laying a solid foundation in Week 1, consider the following personal stories of those who have read this book:

Sarah's Self-Awareness Journey

Sarah, a 32-year-old professional, was plagued with anxiety and self-doubt. She began journaling daily in Week 1 and observed reoccurring negative thought patterns. Now that she knew better, she could challenge these ideas and give way to more positive ones.

Sarah's self-confidence developed with time, and her anxiety decreased dramatically.

John's Achievement in Goal-Setting

During Week 1, John, a college student, set a goal to enhance his physical health by walking for 30 minutes daily. He began little to achieve his goal.

He had fulfilled this objective by the end of the 28-day schedule and observed improved mental clarity and lower stress levels.

Maria's Gratitude Practice

During Week 1, Maria, a mother of two, introduced a thankfulness practice into her everyday routine. She originally found it difficult to focus on the positive aspects of her life while juggling a busy family life.

With time, she learned to appreciate the small pleasures in life, such as her children's laughter and the warmth of her morning coffee. This adjustment in perspective gave her a sense of happiness she hadn't felt in years.

These personal stories show the transforming influence of Week 1's activities and practices. They demonstrate how self-awareness, attainable goals, and basic yet powerful practices may establish the groundwork for substantial personal growth and long-term enjoyment.

CHAPTER FOUR

Week-2: Mindfulness and Self-Compassion

We delve into the profound techniques of mindfulness and self-compassion in the second week of our revolutionary journey to fighting depression and anxiety while unleashing happiness.

Week 2 of your 28-day journey is a turning point in which we focus on improving your emotional well-being through these routines. Let's look at the activities, ideas, and strategies defined for this week.

Week 2 activities include:

Week 2 is about cultivating mindfulness and self-compassion, vital tools for stress management, anxiety reduction, and overall mental well-being. The following are the main activities:

Continue your mindfulness meditation practice, increasing the duration as you feel comfortable.

You'll learn to examine your thoughts and emotions without judgment, improving your ability to stay present.

Self-Compassion Exercise: Practice self-compassion activities to treat oneself with kindness and understanding. These activities will assist you in combating self-criticism and perfectionism.

Mindful Breathing: Throughout the day, practice mindful breathing. During stressful times, take a few moments to pause, focus on your breath, and bring your attention back to the present moment.

Maintain your thankfulness notebook and supplement it with self-compassion. Consider times when you were kind to yourself and recognize them as acts of self-compassion.

The Concept of Mindfulness

Mindfulness is a condition of present-focused awareness that is free of judgment or distraction. It's about completely immersed in whatever you're doing, whether eating, walking in nature, or simply breathing.

Mindfulness helps you to be aware of your thoughts and feelings without attempting to change or judge them.

Consider Emily, a busy worker who practices mindfulness during her daily activities. Instead of fretting about her to-do list or traffic, she concentrates on her breathing and the travel sensations. This simple technique relaxes her mind and lowers her daily stress.

Self-Compassion and Its Importance in Mental Health

Self-compassion is treating oneself with the same love, care, and understanding that one would extend to a close friend during a time of sorrow or difficulty. It entails realizing your humanity, accepting your flaws, and responding to your grief with love and warmth.

For example, James, who began his self-reflection journey in Week 1, discovers the value of self-compassion. He recognizes that punishing himself for previous wrongs only worsens his anxiety. Instead, he responds to his pain with kindness, assuring himself that it's normal to make mistakes and that he deserves to be loved and cared for.

Mindfulness Techniques & Exercises:

Body Scan: Practice a body scan meditation in which you focus on each area of your body, beginning with your toes and working your way up. This practice increases body awareness and relieves physical strain.

Breath Awareness: Pay attention to your breath as it enters and exits your body. Take note of the rise and fall of your chest and the sensation of breath moving through your nose. When your thoughts wander, gently bring them back to the breath.

Loving-Kindness Meditation: Engage in loving-kindness meditation, in which you extend feelings of love and compassion to yourself first, then to loved ones, acquaintances, and even individuals with whom you disagree. This technique promotes self-compassion and good emotions.

Mindful Eating: Pay attention to your food's flavor, texture, and aroma as you savor each bite. Mealtime can be transformed into a mindful, joyful experience by performing this simple act.

Walking Meditation: Practice walking meditation by concentrating on each step as you walk. This exercise, which may be done indoors or outdoors, allows you to incorporate mindfulness into your daily routines.

Self-Compassion Techniques & Exercises:

Positive Self-Talk: Instead of being overly critical or judgmental towards yourself, use positive and supportive language. For example, if you make a mistake, say to yourself, "It's okay; everyone makes mistakes. I can learn from this."

Self-Affirmations: Create and repeat positive affirmations that uplift and encourage you. For instance, "I am worthy of love and happiness," or "I am doing my best, and that is enough."

Mindful Self-Compassion: In moments of difficulty or stress, pause and acknowledge your feelings without judgment. Treat yourself with the same compassion you would offer to a friend going through a similar situation.

Self-Care: Prioritize self-care activities that nurture your emotional, physical, and mental well-being. This can include reading a book or going for a walk-in nature.

Set Realistic Expectations: Avoid setting impossibly high standards for yourself. Understand that it's okay to have limits, and it's not necessary to excel in everything you do.

Forgiveness: Forgive yourself for past mistakes or regrets. Understand that everyone makes errors, and these experiences contribute to growth and learning.

Self-Kindness: Treat yourself with kindness when you're facing challenges. For example, if you're feeling overwhelmed, say to yourself, "I understand this is difficult right now, and I'm here for myself."

Self-Compassion Journaling: Write in a journal about your feelings and experiences, especially during challenging times. Use this as a safe space to express your emotions and offer words of understanding and support to yourself.

Practice Gratitude for Yourself: Reflect on your positive qualities and achievements. Acknowledge your strengths, even if they seem small. Whatever your accomplishments may seem to be, be proud of them.

Create a Self-Compassion Mantra: Develop a personal mantra that reinforces self-compassion. For example, "I am worthy of love and kindness" or "I deserve to be gentle with myself."

CHAPTER FIVE

Week 3: Positive Psychology

We immerse ourselves in the empowering realm of positive psychology during the third week of our 28-day adventure to fight depression and anxiety while unleashing happiness. Week 3 is about delving into the ideas and practices that can inject happiness and well-being into your life. Let's examine the activities, philosophies, and exercises that make up this transformational week.

Week 3 Activities

Week 3 is about accepting and applying positive psychology principles to your daily life. The following are the main activities for this week:

Gratitude Journal: Keep up with your daily gratitude practice of reflecting on and recording three things you're grateful for each evening.

Positive Affirmations: Expand your positive affirmation practice by adding fresh affirmations that boost your confidence and self-esteem.

Positive vision: Practice positive vision exercises in which you imagine your perfect future and the steps necessary to get there. Visualization has been shown to increase motivation and optimism.

Acts of Kindness: Show kindness to others, whether it's a modest gesture or a substantial commitment. These acts not only benefit others but also boost your happiness.

Positive Relationships: Make time in your schedule to cultivate positive relationships. Connect with loved ones, express gratitude, and build your social support network.

Introducing Positive Psychology Principles.

The study of happiness and success is the focus of positive psychology. Rather than focusing exclusively on alleviating suffering, it attempts to discover what makes life meaningful and rewarding. In Week 3, we will expose you to some essential positive psychology principles:

Focus on strength: Positive psychology emphasizes discovering and using one's strengths rather than dwelling on one's faults. Recognizing and exploiting your distinct abilities can lead to a more fulfilling existence.

Positive Emotions: Cultivating good emotions such as gratitude, pleasure, and love can improve general well-being. These emotions serve as stress absorbers, leading to a happier and more resilient mindset.

Optimism: Developing a more optimistic viewpoint on life entails viewing problems as chances for progress and remaining hopeful in facing adversity. Optimism is a skill that can be developed and honed.

Engagement: Positive psychology encourages participation in activities that induce a state of flow—intense focus and delight. Time flies by when you're involved and feel a sense of accomplishment.

The Positive Thinking and Gratitude Effect.

In positive psychology, gratitude and positive thinking are two powerful strategies. They have the power to drastically alter your viewpoint and outlook on life.

Gratitude entails recognizing and appreciating the pleasant parts of your life, whether large or small. This technique redirects your emphasis from what you lack to what you have, cultivating a sense of abundance.

For instance, Sarah, who began her gratitude practice in Week 1, continues to write down what she is grateful for. She finds that she's grown more aware of the beauty in everyday life, from the warmth of the sun on her cheek to her children's laughing. This increased appreciation fills her days with joy and contentment.

Positive thinking entails confronting and replacing negative thought patterns with constructive, hopeful ones. Thinking positively about situations can lessen stress and enhance your mental health.

For example, Emily, who was experiencing workplace stress, began to practice positive thinking. Rather than seeing obstacles as insurmountable, she sees them as chances to learn and grow. This shift in viewpoint alleviates her worry and increases her confidence in dealing with difficult situations.

Practical Positivity Boosting Exercises

Gratitude Journaling: Write a list of things you're grateful for in your gratitude journal and a phrase or two expressing why you're grateful for each. This intensifies and broadens the practice's impact.

Positive Affirmations: List positive affirmations specific to your goals and dreams. Repeat them daily, particularly during times of self-doubt or stress.

Visualization: Spend a few minutes each day picturing a future where you have accomplished your goals and are living a fulfilling life. Consider the specifics—the sights, sounds, and feelings linked with your triumph.

Random Acts of Kindness: During Week 3, complete one random act of kindness daily. It could be as simple as sending a touching message to a friend or assisting a needy stranger. There is a comprehensive act of kindness you can select from. Ensure you select the one convenient with you.

Quality Time: Make time for the excellent relationships in your life. Connect with friends or family members, exchange experiences, and thank them for being there.

How to Comprehensively Carry out visualization

1. Choose a quiet and comfortable space where you won't be disturbed. This can be a corner of your room, a cozy chair, or any place where you can relax.
2. Sit or lie down in a comfortable position. Close your eyes if you're comfortable doing so.
3. Start by inhaling deeply a few times to calm your body and mind. Slowly take a breath in via your nose, hold it for a moment, and then let it out through your mouth.
4. Repeat this several times until you feel relaxed.
5. Begin to picture the future you want to create. Imagine it in as much detail as possible. Consider the following aspects:

6. Visualize the surroundings in your future. What does your environment look like? Where are you? What colors and shapes do you see?

Comprehensive Act of kindness you Could Select

1. You could pay for the person's order behind you in line.
2. Offer a genuine compliment to a stranger, whether it's about their outfit, smile, or something positive you notice.
3. You could donate blood to a local blood bank or participate in a blood drive to help those in need.
4. You could leave uplifting notes or messages in public places like library books, bus stops, or on a colleague's desk.
5. You could offer to mow your elderly neighbor's lawn, shovel their driveway, or assist with household chores.
6. You could give non-perishable food items to a local food bank to help those experiencing food insecurity.

7. Write a heartfelt letter or send a postcard to a friend or family member to brighten their day.

8. On public transportation, offer your seat to someone who needs it more, such as an older adult, pregnant woman, or someone with a disability.

9. Surprise a friend with their favorite treat or coffee when they least expect it.

10. Spend time volunteering at a local shelter, nursing home, or community organization to support those in need.

11. You could declutter your home and donate gently used clothing, toys, or household items to a charity or thrift store.

12. Participate in a tree-planting event to contribute to environmental conservation.

13. Offer a ride to someone without transportation, whether it's a colleague, neighbor, or someone in need.

14. Put out bird feeders in your yard or a local park to provide food for wildlife.

15. Create and send care packages to troops overseas or to someone going through a difficult time.

16. Simple acts like holding the door open for others can go a long way in brightening someone's day.

17. Smile at strangers you pass by on the street. A genuine smile can have a positive impact on someone's mood.

In Week 3, incorporate these practical exercises into your everyday routine to further your understanding of positive psychology and its transforming potential. You can unlock happiness and a full existence by cultivating good emotions, developing optimism, and improving your relationships.

Chapter SEVEN

Week-4 Developing Resilience

We begin building resilience in the fourth and final week of our 28-day journey to fighting depression and anxiety while unlocking happiness. This week is about giving you the tools to recover from setbacks, manage stress, and strengthen your mental health. Let's look at activities, the concept of resilience, and techniques for developing this useful quality, complemented by inspiring stories of people who have overcome adversity.

Week 4 represents the completion of your transformative journey. Here are the main activities you should look forward to throughout this resilience-building week:

Mindful Resilience Techniques: Combine Week 2's mindfulness techniques to increase resilience. Engage in mindfulness meditation focusing on resilience, visualizing yourself conquering obstacles.

Techniques for Stress Reduction: Learn and practice stress-reduction techniques such as regular muscle relaxation and yoga. These techniques will assist you in efficiently managing stress.

Positive Reframing: Investigate cognitive resiliency by practicing positive reframing. This entails looking at difficult situations through a more optimistic and growth-oriented lens.

Stress Journal: Keep a stress journal to track your stressors and patterns. This self-awareness will enable you to make proactive changes to lessen stress.

Support Network: Strengthen your support system by reaching out to friends and family members. Share your experiences and get advice as necessary.

Understanding the Importance of Resilience

Resilience is to bounce back quickly from setbacks, adjust well to changing circumstances, and keep going when the going gets tough.

It is not about avoiding stress but about dealing with it, learning from it, and being stronger.

Resilience is critical in the context of overcoming depression and anxiety. It functions as a shield, lowering vulnerability to mental health difficulties while providing the inner fortitude to address and conquer them.

Coping Strategies for Setbacks and Stress

Positive Self-Talk: Use positive self-talk to combat negative ideas that may occur due to setbacks. Encourage yourself by telling yourself, "I can handle this," or "This too shall pass."

Mindfulness and Relaxation: Include mindfulness and relaxation strategies in your everyday routine, particularly during stressful times. Breathing exercises and meditation can help you quiet your mind and respond more effectively to stress.

Problem Solving: When confronted with a challenge, break it down into smaller, more manageable steps.

Make an action plan to address each part of the problem, and seek help or advice if necessary.

Seeking Help: Don't hesitate to contact your support network when things get tough. Share your thoughts and feelings with friends or family members who can provide advice, comfort, and perspective.

Learn from Adversity: Accept adversity as a source of progress. Consider what you've learned from previous failures and how those experiences have made you stronger and wiser.

Inspiring Resilience Stories

Sarah's Resilience Journey: Sarah, who suffered from severe depression, began her resilience journey by practicing mindfulness meditation. She learned to examine her thoughts and feelings without judgment over time. Because of her newfound strength, she could face her depression with courage. Sarah now lives a fulfilling life and is an inspiration to many.

John's Resilience in the Face of Loss: John suffered a big loss that crushed him. Rather than succumbing, he sought stress-reduction strategies and joined a support group. He took solace in their combined strength and tenacity, eventually mending from his grief and seeking new meaning in his life.

Maria's Strength in Adversity: Maria, a single mother, experienced job loss and financial insecurity. Despite the pressure, she used positive self-talk and resilience techniques. She sought vocational counseling, reevaluated her goals, and eventually found more satisfying employment. Her fortitude helped her financially and motivated her children to face problems with courage and conviction.

These stories demonstrate resilience's transforming power. They show that with persistence, self-compassion, and a willingness to accept help, people can overcome even the most severe hurdles and emerge stronger and more resilient than before.

CHAPTER EIGHT

Maintaining Your Progress

As you near the end of our 28-day journey to fighting depression and anxiety while unlocking happiness, it's critical to remember that your transformation is a continuous process. This chapter will guide you on continuing your journey after the initial 28 days, emphasizing the necessity of ongoing self-care, providing resources and support alternatives, and encouraging you to measure your progress and celebrate your accomplishments.

Extending the Journey

The 28-day journey has given you a solid foundation and transforming skills, but the plan to long-term happiness and mental well-being is continuing. Consider the following ways to preserve and expand on your progress:

Consistency: Maintain the everyday activities and practices you've developed over the last four weeks. Consistency is essential for incorporating positive habits into your everyday routine.

Adapt and evolve: As time passes, your requirements and circumstances may change. Prepare to modify your practices and goals as needed. What works in the first 28 days may need to be tweaked to remain effective.

Set New Goals: As you achieve your initial objectives, set new ones to challenge yourself and further your personal development. These objectives might be tied to any element of your life, from work aspirations to personal connections.

Mindful Awareness: Maintain mindful awareness of your thoughts, emotions, and behaviors. Self-awareness is an ongoing activity that assists you in identifying and addressing potential depression and anxiety triggers.

The Value of Ongoing Self-Care

Self-care is a lifelong commitment to your well-being, not a one-time endeavor. It entails regularly caring for your physical, emotional, and mental health. Here are some of the reasons why ongoing self-care is essential:

Regular self-care routines can aid in the prevention of relapses into sadness and anxiety.

You lower the likelihood of recurrence by continuously managing stress and maintaining emotional equilibrium.

Resilience: Self-care improves resilience, allowing you to recover quickly from setbacks and hardships. It strengthens your mental and emotional reserves.

Quality of Life: Self-care helps to improve one's quality of life. It gives you more joy, satisfaction, and fulfillment in your daily life.

Options for Resources and Assistance

If you found therapy or counseling helpful during the 28-day course, consider continuing it. Sessions with a mental health expert regularly provide continuing guidance and support.

Support Groups: Participating in a support group for depression, anxiety, or other issues can provide a sense of community and understanding. These groups provide a secure environment for people to discuss their experiences and receive encouragement.

Tracking Progress and Celebrating Success:

You can be motivated by monitoring your development and acknowledging your accomplishments. Here's how to do it correctly:

Journaling: Continue to journal your ideas, feelings, and experiences. Consider your journey, noting the obstacles you've faced and the positive changes you've seen.

Milestone Celebrations: Establish and celebrate milestones at regular intervals. These milestones can be weekly, monthly, or yearly. Treat yourself to something special, or express gratitude for your progress.

Share Your Journey: Tell a trustworthy friend or family member about your progress and accomplishments. Declaring your accomplishments aloud might help to reaffirm your commitment and motivation.

Visual Reminders: Make visual representations of your experience.

A vision board, a progress chart, or a collection of encouraging quotes can all be used. These reminders can help you stay focused.

Finally, while the 28-day journey has given you a transforming start, the plan toward long-term happiness and well-being continues. As you continue on your path to personal development, embrace the concepts of consistency, adaptation, and self-care. Remember that you have access to plenty of resources and help, and celebrating your successes will keep you inspired and motivated. Your dedication to your health is a lifelong gift to yourself, and the benefits will continue to accrue as you continue on this joyful journey.

CHAPTER NINE

Overcoming Common Obstacles

In this chapter, we'll address some potential obstacles readers may encounter during their 28-day journey toward defeating depression and anxiety while unlocking happiness. We'll offer practical solutions to common challenges, such as motivation, time management, and setbacks, to help you stay on course.

Motivation: It's natural for motivation to ebb and flow during the 28-day journey. To overcome this challenge:

1. Remind yourself of your reasons for embarking on this journey.
2. Revisit your initial goals and the positive changes you've experienced.
3. If you're having trouble staying motivated, talking to a friend about it or joining a support group might help.

Time Management: Balancing daily activities and the 28-day journey can be challenging. Create a schedule incorporating your daily practices to better manage your time. Prioritize self-care and allocate specific time slots for mindfulness, journaling, and other activities. Consider delegating tasks, when possible, to free up time for your well-being.

Setbacks: Setbacks are a natural part of any transformative journey. If you encounter setbacks, don't be discouraged. Instead, view them as opportunities for growth and resilience. Reflect on what triggered the setback and adjust your strategies accordingly.

Seeking Professional Help: If you find that depression and anxiety persist or worsen despite your efforts, consider seeking professional help. A mental health expert can offer personalized advice and treatment choices. Reaching out for assistance when facing persistent challenges is a sign of strength.

CHAPTER TEN

Conclusion

In Chapter 10, we'll summarize the key takeaways from this book and emphasize the importance of addressing depression and anxiety. We'll encourage you to continue your journey toward happiness and mental health

Key Takeaways

You Have the Power: Throughout this book, we've emphasized that you can defeat depression and anxiety. You can transform your life by cultivating self-awareness, practicing mindfulness, and nurturing positive habits.

Consistency Is Key: Consistent practice is essential for lasting change. The daily activities and practices introduced in this book are tools that, when used consistently, can lead to profound improvements in your mental well-being.

Self-Care Is a Lifelong Commitment: Self-care is not a one-time effort but a lifelong commitment to your well-being. It's a journey that requires ongoing attention and nurturing.

Resilience Matters: Building resilience is crucial. It equips you to face life's challenges with strength and adaptability, reducing vulnerability to depression and anxiety.

Continuing Your Journey

Your 28-day journey is just the beginning. We encourage you to continue practicing the techniques and principles you've learned. Set new goals, deepen your mindfulness practice, and nurture your resilience. Your commitment to your well-being is a lifelong gift to yourself.

A Message of Hope and Inspiration

In closing, we want to offer a message of hope and inspiration. It's possible to overcome depression and anxiety; your journey proves your strength and resilience. You can live a happy, fulfilling life filled with purpose and joy.

Remember that asking for assistance does not indicate weakness but strength. You are never alone on this journey; support and guidance are available. Surround yourself with a network of friends, family, and professionals who can assist you on your path to well-being.

As you continue your journey, remember that setbacks are growth opportunities, and every step forward is a victory. Embrace each day with mindfulness, self-compassion, and optimism. You can unlock happiness and mental health; we believe in your thriving ability.

With determination and self-care, you can overcome common challenges, find peace, and build a brighter future. Your story is one of strength, resilience, and transformation worth celebrating.

www.ingramcontent.com/pod-product-compliance
Lightning Source LLC
Chambersburg PA
CBHW031330250726

48656CB00005B/2063